The Suicide Prevention Family Handbook

A New Approach to Loved Ones with Depression, Overcoming Ideation, and Life After Loss

PREFACE

This handbook developed over the last 20 years. In 2003, I helped my first client release the emotional pain fueling her suicidal ideation, and the issue resolved on the spot. Over the next 15 years, clients would occasionally express suicidal thoughts. I approached those situations in the same way and saw the same results.

In 2015, I published, *3 Keys to Managing PTSD*, and began applying my process with more veterans. With each call, my learning went deeper.

In 2019, I partnered with National Veteran Resources during their Mission 22 - 0 tours across the country. I functioned as an on-call suicide prevention specialist helping the most high-risk veterans they met. I continued to learn from each conversation.

In 2023, I was invited by the commissioner of the NYC Department of Veterans' Services to share our offerings at The Military Transition Summit at Citi Field. This is where I met the COO of Black Veterans for Social Justice. He asked if I can create a mindfulness-based suicide prevention protocol and train their crisis team how to use it.

This had been a dream of mine. I created a flowchart and script illustrating how I was saving lives and the Stress Is Gone Suicide Prevention Protocol was born. Three months later I trained my first vet-to-vet crisis team. I continue to train suicide prevention specialists in the protocol, online and in-person.

TABLE OF CONTENTS

INTRODUCTION

I wrote this handbook to provide a step-by-step guide to help people who: *(1) have loved ones suffering from depression, (2) are experiencing suicidal thoughts themselves, and (3) wish to reopen their hearts to feel emotionally reconnected with their lost loved ones.*

Often, when a family member expresses suicidal ideation it elicits a stress reaction within the person listening. This reaction usually makes matters worse for the depressed person. Emotional pain arises to be seen, heard, and loved. If we do these three things emotional pain releases naturally. This book shows you how to hold space for someone's healing by listening with compassion.

While coaching people suffering from suicidal ideation, I noticed their support system was often misaligned. Typically people want support from those who can't give it, and overlook support from those who can. This book helps you properly reset your support system and set up your daily calendar to prioritize your personal healing.

While coaching those who have lost loved ones that passed from suicide, I have seen as they let go of pain the relationship begins to reframe. As this happens my client's heart begins to reopen and reconnect with their loved one emotionally, spiritually, and in dreams.

Before we get started, please complete the support system chart below. Use it as challenging feelings arise. For assistance with this material, call us for coaching.

	Family	Friends	Mental Health Pro.	Stress Is Gone
Name				Brett Cotter
Phone				833-867-3529
Name				
Phone				

CHAPTER 1
Helping Loved Ones with Depression

I remember the fear I felt in 2003 like it was yesterday, because I knew the words were on the way, and then I heard her say, "I don't want to be here anymore. I want to end it all today."

After 25 years of helping people heal from the most traumatic events of their lives, I have learned a few important lessons about our emotions:

1. *Emotional pain releases when it's seen, heard, and loved. All pain wants is love. When a person is met with compassion, kindness, and connection, their defenses drop.*
2. *If a person feels safe, they become vulnerable, which allows the source of their pain to arise to the surface.*
3. *If the source of a person's pain is seen, heard, and loved, it too will release.*

The two challenges to overcome that continually interrupt the emotional healing process are: Loved ones often automatically overreact from stress and cannot greet this pain with love. The person in pain identifies with the rising emotion and holds on to it as it tries to release.

Imagine what it will feel like as you and your family overcome both these challenges by practicing the techniques in this book. The most important thing to remember is that all painful emotions are coming up to be released.

"I was going through intense stress and anxiety about our daughter's well-being. Thank you for providing a safe space for my body, mind, and spirit to be unburdened, lifted, and lightened. I felt transformed. I am deeply grateful for the healing life force energy I am able to access within my own body."

- Licia Thomas, Therapist

3 Keys to Deliver Effective Support

The words your stress wants to say will not help your loved one's pain go away.

Holding space is an ability to be present as a compassionate listener without judgment or reacting while someone else is expressing their emotional pain.

Effectively holding space for a loved one suffering with depression or suicidal ideation is not easy but it is possible and essential to foster a safe, loving, and healing environment.

Release Your Stress to Hold Space for Theirs

1. *Become aware when your stress is triggered.*
2. *Release the stress before it expresses itself.*
3. *Return to the present moment.*

1. Become Aware When Your Stress is Triggered
Pay attention to your body during the conversation. You are stressed the moment you:

- Are upset emotionally
- Feel tension build anywhere in your body
- Notice your heart rate or breath rate increase
- Start thinking negatively

2. Release Your Stress Before It Expresses Itself
Embrace your emotion with your breath by: Touching the tension and breathing deeply and slowly into the tightness.

3. Return to the Present Moment
Silently say these mantras once per breath to remain calm:
• *I'm okay. We're okay. I love you.*

How To Hold Space For Your Loved One

1. Become Aware When Your Stress is Triggered

2. Release Your Stress Before It Expresses Itself

3. Return to the Present Moment

Compassionate Body Language & Tone

Only 7% of human communication is through spoken words. The remaining 93% is conveyed through body language and tone.

How to Express Compassion with Body Language

1. Position: Face to face, at arm's distance or closer.

2. Posture: Left side slightly forward, limbs uncrossed.

3. Hands: Left hand slightly forward on left thigh, palm facing up, use a gentle touch during intense moments.

4. Face & Eyes: Soft expressions, occasional slight raise of eyebrows, maintain eye contact, look into their right eye with your left eye.

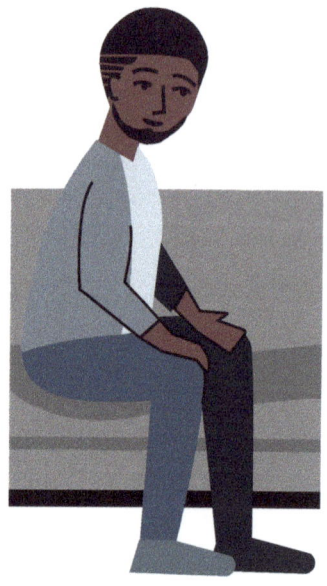

Don'ts: Cross limbs, touch your face, fidget, look shocked, move around, wave arms excessively.

(Mehrabian, A., 1981. Silent Messages. Belmont, Calif.: Wadsworth Pub.)

How to Exude Compassion with Your Tone

1. Speak softly: Allows defenses to subside.

2. Speak slowly: Allows the central nervous system to settle down.

3. Use a low pitch: Ground your pitch by placing your right hand on your belly button and taking deep slow breaths. This will elicit calmness in the body.

4. Mirroring: During intense moments halfway match their tone so they know you are listening and are connected to what they are saying.

Don'ts: Speak in a high or changing pitch, speak quickly, speak loud, speak in a monotone voice.

Proper use of body language helps your loved one feel safe enough to let their deepest pain arise.

How to Help a Loved One Open Up

Knowing what to say helps your stress melt away.

The biggest fear among all the suicide prevention specialists I have trained was losing someone because they didn't know what to say. Fear creates stress that compounds the other person's pain.

Knowing What to Say

First we must understand our role: to provide a safe space for the other person to express the layers of their emotions and release the depths of their pain.

Your role is not to solve their problems. It's to see, hear, and love the person as they express their pain.

The 5 Prompts

We use 5 Prompts in the SIG Suicide Prevention Protocol to help callers, clients, and patients open up and express their feelings. Now you can use this to help your loved one.

1. *Please tell me more.*
2. *I want to hear everything.*
3. *What's the hardest part to talk about?*
4. *What's your biggest fear about that?*
5. *What does that feel like?*

How to Use the 5 Prompts Most Effectively

1. Proper body language and tone the entire time.
2. After stating a prompt be quiet and listen.
3. Release your stress and be present as you listen.
4. When they're done talking ask the next prompt.
5. Stick to the sequence and cycle through the prompts again after the core pain surfaces.

9

How to Listen

Instead of words, respond with body language cues so the other person has more space to express their pain. Expression is the path to emotional freedom.

Being a Good Listener Takes:

- Self-awareness to know when your stress is triggered by what you just heard.

- Self-regulation skills to know how to quickly release stress from your body so you can continue to listen. The easiest way is to touch the tension, breathe deep and slow, and once per breath silently say, *"I'm okay."* If the other person asks why you are touching your heart, solar plexus, or stomach, you can say, *"I really feel what you're saying right now."*

- Mental focus to pay attention to what the other person is saying and how they are saying it.

- Knowledge of body language concepts to help the other person feel comfortable.

Being a good listener boils down to clearing your mind of thoughts so you can witness theirs. You are holding space as their emotions express, unravel, and release.

As the layers of their pain arise you experience an internal back-and-forth between releasing your own stress and being fully present for their's.

The act of listening creates a bond that fosters trust and connection between both individuals.

Connect and Co-regulate

Once the connection is firmly established through listening, the individual's core pain unravels and co-regulation begins. Now the listener plays an active role in comforting and grounding the other person.

After slowly moving through the 5 Prompts the core pain should be on the surface. Now we strengthen the connection between the two of you. Intuitively choose a few of the statements below that feel right in the moment.

Statements to Solidify Your Connection

- *We are in this together.*

- *I'm not going anywhere.*

- *I'm right here with you.*

- *Thank you so much for sharing this with me.*

- *I am so sorry; I had no idea it hurt this bad.*

- *You did such a great job expressing all this to me.*

Co-Regulate with Them

- Gently take their hands in yours.

- Look into their eyes and silently say, "I love you."

- Breathe deep and slow, repeat the "I love you" mantra once per breath until your heart opens.

- Bring them in for a hug so their head is near your left shoulder (so you are heart to heart).

- Continue breathing deep and slow, saying the mantra aloud, allowing your hearts to connect.

- When you both are calm slowly break the hug.

- Ask them to touch the tension in their body, breathe deeply and slowly, and once per breath say aloud, *"I unlock and release all this tension right now."*

- Have them slowly repeat the above statement until the tension releases.

Summary

I remember the fear I felt in 2003 like it was yesterday. I knew the words were on the way, and then I heard her say, "I don't want to be here anymore. I want to end it all today."

Now I'll share with you the rest of that story. After I recognized my own fear, I embraced it by touching the tension and breathing into my emotions. The fear quickly released, and I was able to reset into the present moment. With love and compassion, I said, "Please tell me more." She opened up; we got below the pain to what felt like an endless sea of inner peace for both of us. Twenty plus years later, she is a beloved massage therapist in her community.

We can witness someone rise from the depths of their pain if we get out of the way by releasing our own stress and remaining present. The present moment is like a window that opens to pure consciousness and has the power to return chaos to calmness. We use body language to deliver the 5 Prompts and listen. We avoid wordy responses to provide more space for the other person to express their pain. Finally, we connect and co-regulate.

It's important to remember every soul that comes to this planet has its' own path, purpose, challenges, lessons to learn, and destiny.

We are in this together.

Extra Resources for Worst-Case Scenarios

To eliminate the stress of saying or doing the wrong thing, below are two components from our Suicide Prevention Protocol adjusted to support a loved one. You will most likely never have to use the below resources. **I am including them so you have the tools to handle the situation should it arise.**

Risk Assessment

If you feel a loved one might be in danger of hurting themselves or someone else, ask these questions:

Do you feel like you're in danger of harming yourself or anyone else right now?

Do you have means to do so?

Have you made a plan?

Have you started preparing?

Did you tell anyone?

If yes, call 911

* DIAL 988 for mental health urgencies and 911 for mental health emergencies.

Keep a Person Engaged Until Help Arrives

If a loved one is considering acting on their ideation use these statements after 911 is dispatched.

- **Don't worry about 911. This happens every day** to thousands of good people. It's just one moment, and we're going to get through it. The craziness of the world really hurts good-hearted people. The world is crazy, you're not. Just stick with me and breathe with me. I love you. We'll get through this together.

- **I promise you, once we get the right support in place, everything will stabilize** and you'll feel better. I believe in you. Just a little more time. Stick with me. Breathe with me. I love you.

- If you think everyone is better off without you, **let's call the rest of the family right now to see what they say.**

- **Right now, you're emotionally injured.** In many ways, it's worse than a physical injury because there's no surgery or stitches to make this pain go away. I am here with you. The way we get through this is together. Just touch the tension in your body and breathe deeply and slowly with me. I love you. I got you.

- **STOP! All this pain is not the real you**; it's passing through you. I'll prove it to you. Have you felt all this pain every waking moment of your entire life? No. It's not the real you; it's actually opposite, that's why it hurts so much. Yes, the pain is unbearble, but it's only temporary. I promise you, we will get through this together. Breathe with me. Stick with me. I love you.

- **STOP! I hear you, and I am all in with you.** I am right here with you, and if I went through what you went through I'd feel the exact same way you do. I love you. Now stick with me and breathe with me. This pain is temporary. I promise you.

- **STOP! Your life was not a waste** because we all love you, and we'd be devastated without you, and you don't know what's waiting for you on the other side. You might have to come right back and go through all this pain again just to get past this very point in your soul's journey. So let's get past it together right now. I promise you, I am here with you now. I love you. Stick with me. Breathe deeply and slowly with me.

- **Every cell on this planet is programmed to return to stability** (scientifically it's called homeostasis). I know it doesn't feel like it right now, but everything's going to be stable again. I promise you. Let's just get through this moment together. Breathe with me. I love you.

- **Yes this pain is unbearable, but it's not the real you.** I promise you it's only temporary even though it feels like eternity. Breathe with me. Deeply and slowly. I love you. We will make it through.

- **It's not your fault; it's just a cycle** that started from all the built up stress that turned into anxiety, then overwhelm, then hopelessness, then depression, and now the desire to not be here anymore. That's how this happened. We're going to unravel it step by step in the opposite direction. We're breaking this cycle together. It's not your fault. Stick with me. Breathe with me.

- **I know you're in pain, and people don't get it**; the support hasn't been there, and that's not fair, but that's changing right now. At the end of your rope is when you find that thing that's bigger than you, that's been looking out for you the entire time. Now we are getting through this moment together. Follow me, touch the tension in your body, and breathe deeply and slowly with me. I will see you through this. I love you.

- **I don't blame you for wanting to go. I know the pain is unbearable. Even though you want to, I'm just saying not to.** Because I love you and the right help is right around the corner for you. This pain is passing I promise you. Now touch the tension in your body. Breathe with me, nice and easy, deeply and slowly.

- **No wait; I can't lose you. I heard everything you said, and I am all in with you.** I care way too much about you. We're in this together. You can't leave me because I'm not leaving you. Just stay with me one more moment. Touch the tension in your body. Breathe deeply and slowly, and say this right after me, "I unlock and release this pain from my body right now!" (Let them repeat aloud.) Yes, now breathe right into the center of the tension inside your body. That's it, stick with me. Say it again right after me, "I unlock and release all this pain from my body right now!" (Let them repeat aloud.) Yes, now imagine breathing deeper and slower right through the tightness inside your body. Yes, keep breathing. Imagine the tension releasing. We got this. I love you.

- **STOP! it's a default;** this is the brain's way out of deep emotional pain. There's another way. Stay with me. I promise you we will make it through, I love you.

CHAPTER 2
New Approach to Recover from Ideation

I remember the pain I felt in 2008 upon realizing I was losing the custody case for my son. He was resting on my chest, and I was agonizing over the situation. I closed my eyes and had a vision of ending my life. The scariest part was the relief I felt while seeing that vision.

My dad used to say, *"There's a tool for every job."* I took that to mean, anything is possible with the right tool. In this chapter, I hand you a flashlight to find your way out of the darkness.

All mental illness starts with matters of the heart. Even where science says it's genetic or hereditary, I say check the ancestry, and you will see it all started with unresolved matters of the heart.

I was teaching a monthly class at a clinic for adults diagnosed with schizophrenia, bipolar disorder, borderline personality disorder, etc. When the group's stress level dropped from a 9 out of 10, to a 3, something special happened. Clinic staff joined our sessions, as the patients they served now had less stress than the mental health professionals around them.

"When I first came in contact with Brett I was angry, depressed, suicidal, and above all I trusted no one. In approximately 45 minites that all changed, I followed his lead. I have learned how to cope with PTSD and be at peace within myself. I owe my life to Brett and Stress Is Gone. Thank you brother."

– Rick Williamson, Army Veteran, Peer Support Specialist

A Holistic Perspective on Ideation

Suicidal Ideation is normal in our crazy world. No one showed us how to manage or release all the stress we innocently absorbed as children from our family, school, and community. When we were young, stress happened to us. Now stress happens through us.

Suicidal Ideation

Thoughts of suicide is the brain's logical response to extended periods of physical or emotional pain.

Our brain is like a supercomputer, always problem solving but depressive beliefs (e.g., "it's never going to get better") and behaviors (e.g., lying in bed all day) stop the supercomputer from doing its job. Depressive beliefs and behaviors quickly shut down all solutions.

Stress-Ideation Cycle

Ideation results when stress goes unchecked and forms anxiety, which then forms overwhelm, which turns into hopelessness, and then depression. If the depression doesn't lift, ideation is the brain's way out.

For the last 20 years, suicidal ideation has been on the rise. Our body is the library storing the stress of our ancestors inside our cellular memory. These deep emotions get stirred up every time our stress gets triggered. Your feelings are not your fault, but they are yours to fix by embracing, expressing, and loving them.

For the past 2,500+ years, the Hindu tradition has believed in chakras. The heart chakra spins and radiates energy outward. I believe depression reverses the spin creating an inward vortex and heaviness on the chest.

4 Keys to a Great Support System

While coaching clients through periods of ideation, I noticed an aspect of their support system was off, which intensified their ideation. Specifically, wanting love and support from people who couldn't give it, while overlooking support from those who could. It's a pattern like repeatedly sticking a fork in an electrical outlet, emotionally shocking ourselves every time. This may stem from an unmet parental need from childhood.

A great support system has the right people in the right place. If you need a plumber to fix your sink, you don't call an electrician. If you want emotional support, rely on the good listeners in your life and build your support system around them.

1st Key to a Great Support System

The right family member(s). Choose someone who gets you, that listens, and that feels comforting to talk to. Not someone who is overreactive, goes into their story, or tells you how you should feel. Those people in your life are not bad, they just aren't helpful right now.

2nd Key to a Great Support System

The right friend(s). Not all friends are able to show empathy. Some friends avoid having deep emotional conversations. Let your friends know you are going through a really rough time and you could use some emotional support with check-in phone calls, visits, etc. Select one or two friends who get you, can listen, and are comforting to connect with. Temporarily setting aside friends who cannot listen, hold space, or spend quality time with you is beneficial for your recovery.

3rd Key to a Great Support System

The right team of mental health professionals.

The right psychiatrist is the top person in your city who is involved in studies or clinics for depression. They often run tests before prescribing or changing medications, as they know it's a high-risk time.

The right therapist has years experience treating depression and a clear approach for reducing ideation. I recommend 2+ sessions per week until ideation stops.

The right coach has strong experience helping people move through periods of depression to a place of more self-compassion, trust, and love.

Finding your team through referrals by asking friends and family that work in a related field (such as pharmaceutical sales), *"Who is the top psychiatrist in the area that treats depression?"* You can also ask people that were in therapy, *"Who is the best therapist you recommend?"* Another way is searching online for lists of top local professionals by title and then reading their Yelp and Google reviews.

4th Key to a Great System

The most important key is - **YOU!** You have instant access to your thoughts, actions, and weekly calendar.

Inside-Out Approach helps you release the fear that fuels the depression. We discuss this in the next section.

Outside-In Approach involves spending 10 minutes each day singing and dancing to your three favorite songs. Ideally barefoot outside in the sunlight when you feel most depressed. Also, take 10 minutes each night to touch the tension, and breathe deep and slow. Each week, attend two outside events, with other people, that might be fun.

Respond to Stress Effectively

The first step is using stress signals to become aware when our body becomes anxious, depressed, or stressed.

5 Stress Signals are feeling emotionally upset, thinking negative thoughts, a fast heart rate, an increased breath rate, and physical tension in our body. Once we become aware our body is stressed, we observe it.

4 Tips to Observe Your Stress are listen to your thoughts as if you're listening to the radio. Watch tension build in your body as if you're watching TV. Sit with your emotions as if you're sitting with an old friend. And lastly, have compassion for your feelings as if you're consoling a young child.

3 Steps to Release Stress Fast
1. Touch the emotional tension with both hands.
2. Close your eyes, breathe deeply and slowly.
3. Once per breath, say, *"I'm alive"*, and on the next full breath say, *"I'm okay."*

Repeat step 3 until the tension releases. You may hear a flood of negative thoughts; stay focused on the technique and the negative thoughts will release once the tension unlocks from your body. This could take 20 minutes, so get comfortable and be patient.

Find Your Favorite Mantra for Step 3.
- *I love when the tension releases.*
- *I can remember what love feels like.*
- *I love remembering what love feels like.*
- *I remember what love feels like.*
- *Thank you for making it easier.*

Release Anxiety Quickly

Anxiety differs from stress in that it often arises from within without a clear external stress trigger. Anxiety stems from accumulated stress and is fueled by a subconscious fear. As we surface and release the deeper fear the anxiety clears.

IMPORTANT Only use the following exercise with your therapist as surfacing your core fear is extremely triggering and professional support is necessary.

Anxiety Freedom Technique is a three step process to surface and release your subconscious fear to regain calmness and clarity.

 **Step 1** Surface the Subconscious Fear

A List the 4 biggest stressors in your life right now and circle the most upsetting one:

B What is the worst-case scenario of the stress you circled?

C What is your biggest fear about that worst-case scenario?

D Where do you feel tension in your body while thinking about this core fear?

📣 **Step 2** Fill in Your Freedom Statement using your answers from **Step 1.**

"I unlock and release all the tension from my [insert **D***]*

and completely break free from the fear of [insert **C***]*

right now!"

Step 3. Release the Anxiety.

1 Lie down on your back comfortably. Touch the area of your body where you feel the emotional tension. If you can't reach it, focus your attention on that area.

2 Slowly read your Freedom Statement while breathing deeply and slowly for 10-minutes or until you feel the tension release from your body.

3 Place one hand on your heart and the other hand on your belly button. Breathe deep and slow. Once per breath silently say, *"I'm ok."* Close your eyes and continue for 10-minutes or until you feel at peace.

If you are having trouble releasing the tension or feeling at

peace after 20 minutes, try one of the below approaches. Only proceed to the next approach if the current one does not help you feel relaxed. Take your time.

Replace the "I" at the beginning of your Freedom Statement with your favorite word to refer to your higher power and insert the word "me" before the word "free." Then repeat **Step 3** with the adjusted Freedom Statement.

Touch the emotional tension in your body. Breathe deeply and slowly, imagining the airflow moving through the center of the tension inside you. Start expressing how you are feeling; state which emotion the tension feels like, and openly express what that emotion wants to say.

Go back and look at your answer for **Step 1**, Part **C**. *What is the worst-case scenario of your answer and what's your biggest fear about it?*

Then rewrite your Freedom Statement and redo **Step 3**.

Challenge Negative Thoughts Successfully

Your brain is an antenna, receiving thoughts from infinite sources in and around you. When your body gets stressed, fearful thoughts and emotions hijack your consciousness. Those worrisome thoughts are not you; they are your body's way of trying to survive. Before we go any further, here are a few simple exercises to get you thinking about the mind-body-spirit relationship. Are you the car or the driver? The weeds or the gardener?

Exercise 1: Close your eyes and imagine moving your right arm in some way. Now open your eyes, look at your right arm, and move it in that way.

Are you your body or the thing that decides how to move it?

Exercise 2: Silently repeat three times, *"I am here right now."* Were you able to hear your inner voice?

If yes, could anyone else hear what you said?

If no, what does that mean to you regarding the inner and outer world?

Exercise 3: Follow along with this Q&A sequence.

Q - What are you?

A - A human being.

Q - What happens to your body when you leave it?

A - My body decomposes and returns to the earth.

Q - If it decomposes when you die, what do you bring to your body while you are alive in it?

A - A life-force energy, a spirit.

Q - What are you?

In summary, I hope these exercises encouraged you to think: maybe you're not the mind or the body. Maybe you're something far greater that can observe both.

Making it this far is success in itself. Your effort through the struggle is the victory, and facing these challenges is part of your soul's journey. Whatever happens from here on out, no judgment because even though you may not feel like it yet, you are a champion and you inspire me. Approach this part like a game, with childlike curiosity.

Get Binary with All Your Thoughts

This is where you become like an accountant or an auditor. I want you to be very aware of your thoughts being positive or negative. Think in terms of 1's or 0's, X's and O's, Yes's or No's, Flowers or Weeds, etc. No negative thought slips by without being challenged.

Becoming Conscious of Your Negative Thoughts

On the next page, write down your most repetitive negative thoughts and the opposite or reverse thought. For example,

REPETITIVE NEGATIVE THOUGHT	OPPOSITE / REVERSE THOUGHT
I can't do this.	We did it.
Nothing is working.	Everything is effortless.
I feel like I'm losing my mind.	I know I found my feelings.
It's never going to change.	Everything always changes.
It's never going to be better.	It's getting better right now.
I want to be alone.	We all want to be together.
There's no point in going on.	There's infinite reasons to live.
Everyone's better off w/o me.	I'm better off with everyone.
My life was a waste.	Our life is a gift.

REPETITIVE NEGATIVE THOUGHT	OPPOSITE / REVERSE THOUGHT

How to Challenge Your Negative Thoughts

Now that you are aware of your repetitive negative thoughts, every time you hear one, challenge it immediately. Touch the tension in your body, breathe deep and slow, and, once per breath, say aloud the opposite or reverse thought. Also, imagine the airflow moving through the center of the tightness in your body, as you challenge negative thoughts.

3 Approaches to Challenge Negative Thoughts

Laughingly: Greet the negative thought with an inner chuckle and then say the opposite or reverse thought.

Firmly: Greet the negative thought with authority and say, *"I take all my power back from that thought right now."* Then say the opposite or reverse thought.

Spiritually: Greet the negative thought with your higher power and say, "Thank you, higher power for releasing that negativity from every aspect of me right now." Then say the opposite or reverse thought.

Summary

I remember the pain I felt in 2008 upon realizing I was losing the custody case for my son. He was resting on my chest, and I was agonizing over the situation. I closed my eyes and had a vision, of ending my life. The scariest part was the relief I felt while seeing that vision.

Now for the rest of that story. When I felt the relief from seeing the vision I knew I was in really bad shape and immediately called a therapist. For me, she was more like the oracle in the movie The Matrix. I told her what I wanted to do and she said, "Do you want me to smack you? You have too much important work to do." I was shocked, but those words did something for me. They woke me up inside. Keep in mind, I grew up with the very tough and powerful love of my mother, so this was how I received love. I've never used those words with clients, but I have heard similar stories from my peers that sometimes spontaneous, irreverent, or intuitive responses can crack the code of ideation.

The things to remember here are:

- *The world is crazy; you are not, and*
- *You are not your thoughts.*

Answers to these two questions arise from within and ground you on this planet over time; *"What am I?"* and *"What is my soul's purpose for coming here?"*

"Battling depression, anxiety and PTSD for decades led me to several counselors but Brett was different. His technique guided me through the exact healing I needed. It didn't take long at all! I say he is a miracle worker and I am the miracle!"

– Rhonda Stockstill, Ret. U.S. Air Force

Our life is a gift.

CHAPTER 3
A New Approach to Life After Loss

I remember the fear I felt when facilitating my first workshop for the Mothers of Veteran Suicide. The heaviness began to twist in my chest as I faced the endless abyss of sorrow, loss, and complex PTS. Silently, I thought, "My God, how is the light going to shine through this?"

Over the years, I began to see similarities in those who returned to the flow of life after the tragedy of losing a loved one. The first similarity is a deep personal decision, like arriving at a fork in the road, where one decides, "Yes, I am ready to let go of some of this pain."

The second similarity is that they allow me to coach them through expressing the unspeakable pain. This creates new space to reopen their heart and mind, and restores the connection with the unconditional love they are made of, far beyond space and time.

The third similarity is a renewed sense of purpose in one's life. Finding a new, fulfilling, and meaningful purpose allows happiness and love to slowly return into one's life.

"My son was a disabled Marine veteran that died by suicide. Brett has been instrumental in me moving forward and raising my grandson. After a session I was wrapped in the warmth, love and presence of my son, grandma, and grandpa. It was so peaceful. This happened again after another session and I felt my son with me all day. Brett is a guiding light and I don't know how I would have moved forward without his help!"

– Sandra Henderson, Retired, Arkansas

Being Ready to Heal

This is a tough decision because our pain bonds to the memory of the person we lost. Please know you are not letting go of the person; you are letting go of the pain. As you heal emotionally, you reopen your heart to feel the unconditional love you are both made of.

Reopening Your Heart

If you are ready to release deep emotional pain, I recommend using a Stress Is Gone Coach because I know how well it works. If you are unable to use out-of-network services, you can use the *3 Keys to Reopen Your Heart*. Before proceeding, have your support system handy. We discussed this on page 1 and 23, as this work is very tough; you process extremely deep feelings, and you will cry. Part of the healing process is realizing you are okay even when you're crying.

3 Keys to Reopen Your Heart

1st Key: *Practice letting the tears flow to let the pain go.* Every time you hold back your tears, you hold back your healing. Losses further from the heart may take hundreds of tears to process the pain, while losses closer to the heart can take thousands.

Allow yourself to go through the emotional carwash; it's a necessary part of our healing process. As we allow space for the tears our perception clears. Our lifetime consists of two things: life and time. While on this planet, we are meant to live, and the universe knows exactly when and how to heal us.

I encourage you to surrender your feelings real-time as they arise. You can start with these mantras: *"It's safe to let myself cry," "It's time to let myself cry," "Crying is part of the process," "Even though it hurts, I'm okay,"* and *"These tears and fears will pass."*

🪶 **2nd Key:** *Express the depths of your pain as it arises.* Every time you feel sad or heartbroken, I want you to:

1. Touch the tension in your body (usually your heart).

2. Breathe deeply and slowly into the tightness.

3. Express your feelings openly. Start by saying:

a. Right now, I feel so [write which emotion]

b. I feel it in my [write where the tension is]

c. This pain is about [write name of the deceased]

d. The hardest thing to say is [finish sentence]

e. What I'm dreading the most is, [finish sentence]

4. "[Say your word for your higher power] unlock and release this [insert 3a]

from my [insert 3b]

and break me free from the fear of [insert 3e]

right now." Repeat steps **1-2-4** until the tension releases.

3rd Key: *Reframe the relationship.* Another extremely important personal decision is whether you let the relationship with your loved one fully transition from the physical world to a more emotional and spiritual relationship and connection. Also, do you want your relationship to be defined by the love you are both made of or the circumstances of their passing? If you choose to reframe the relationship with love, you can;

- Talk to them as if they are standing in front of you every time they come to mind.

- When going to sleep, place two hands on your heart and repeat this mantra, "I'm okay here", take a full breath, "(insert loved one's name) is okay over there," take a full breath, "We are all okay."

Repeat until you fall asleep and again when you first wake up in the morning. This strengthens new neural pathways in your brain and wires them into your heart.

New Perspective on Guilt

Every soul has its own path, purpose, challenges, and lessons to learn in this life. No matter what we want those to be for another person, it doesn't change what is. When souls come and go from this world, there is a covenant between that soul and the creator. Often, the universe uses those around us to facilitate the process.

After someone passes, we automatically second-guess what we did and said, torturously trying to figure out if we could have done something better to prolong their life. This is an automatic survival mechanism in our DNA. Mammals learn how to survive when they see others die. It's not your fault. There is a much bigger picture then what our eyes see, and it may be your time to let go.

Unconditional love operates beyond the barriers of time and space. As you forgive the unforgivable, accept the unacceptable, and love the unloveable within yourself, your heart reopens through the infinite power of self-love. Every time you use one of the 3 Keys to Reopen Your Heart, you are experiencing self-love.

A few questions to help put guilt in perspective are;

- *Would your loved one want you to live with guilt or be completely free and happy?*

- *Does holding on to the guilt help anybody?*

- *What would your life be like without this guilt?*

Remember, our loss is always heaven's gain. This is not the last stop on the soul train. You will see them again.

Mind-Body-Spirit Connection

Let's revisit the below three exercises from chapter two, in hope of further expanding your beliefs around the mind-body-spirit connection.

Exercise 1: Close your eyes and imagine moving your right arm in some way. Now open your eyes, look at your right arm, and move it in that way.

Are you your body or the thing that decides how to move it?

Exercise 2: Silently repeat three times, "I am here right now."
Were you able to hear your own voice say it?
If yes, could anyone else hear what you said?
If no, what does that mean to you, regarding the inner and outer world?

Exercise 3: Follow along with this Q&A sequence.

Q - What are you?

A - I am a human being.

Q - What will happen to your body when you leave it?

A - My body will return to the earth as it decomposes.

Q - If it decomposes when you die, what do you bring to your body while you are alive in it?

A - I bring a life-force energy, a spirit.

Q - So what are you truly?

I hope these exercises help you think differently. From solely identifying with the body to seeing you and your loved ones as pure life-force energy. This energy can neither be created nor destroyed; it changes form as we move from the temporary world into eternity.

Letting Go with Love Visualization

This exercise can be used as a visualization while looking out of a sunlit window or a meditation using your imagination to experience all 6 steps.

1. Standing in front of a window with open arms breathing deeply and slowly, feeling the sunlight.

2. Noticing a bird flying towards you from the direction of the sun.

3. Reaching out allowing a white dove to land in the palms of your hands.

4. Holding the dove closely to your chest, as your heart radiates more love, with each passing breath.

5. Opening your hands to let the dove go, as it takes flight into a beam of pure sunlight.

6. Imagining the dove disappears in the distance, as you breathe and receive eternal sunlight.

The dove symbolizes your loved one and the sunlight is the unconditional love you are both made of.

Calling Loved Ones Into Our Dreams

If a loved one lived next door and every time you stopped by they immediately cried uncontrollably, how often would you visit? Probably not often, and if you really cared about them, maybe never. This is why I want you to heal your heartache. As you reopen your heart you can use the below process to invite your loved ones into your dreams.

This is exactly what I did after my dad passed and he's come to me in over 35 dreams since he passed. I was heartbroken, often going to sleep and waking up crying, until I started using the *3 Keys to Reopen Your Heart* with the below technique.

When going to sleep I would:

1. Close my eyes and say my nighttime affirmations to reframe the relationship until I was calm.

2. Next, I would recite these words exactly: *"Thank you universe, for having (insert loved one's full name) come to me in tonight's dreams so I can remember them in the morning."*

3. Finally, I would return to my reframing affirmations breathing deeply and slowly with two hands on my heart until I fell asleep.

I find when my dad visits me in dreams, they would end quickly if I cried uncontrollably or asked him, "Where are you living now?" or "How is heaven?" When I went with the flow of the dream it was always an incredible loving experience.

Other Ways Our Loved Ones Contact Us

There are infinite ways our relatives can reach us. It's just a matter of being open. That's why step 1 is always going to be healing the heartache. Once you let go of the bulk of the pain they will start contacting you if you want them to.

Nature: Every time an animal or insect shows up in an odd, unique, or special way I want you to Google "Native American Totem (insert the type of animal or insect here), meaning." There are times a bird, squirrel, or insect would be knocking at my window as if they had a message for me. Now I know they do, and now you can interpret those messages too.

Thoughts, Feelings, and Memories: I feel our relatives can easily connect with us through our thoughts. Think of the random thoughts that come to mind like the new text messages and the deep feelings are like phone calls. Random memories that come to mind can also be our loved ones knocking at the door, patiently waiting for us to answer.

Live Radio: If you are emotionally processing listen to live radio stations. Sometimes our relatives put in requests that speak to our soul and help us let go.

Numbers: If you notice certain numbers repeatedly appearing thoughout your day; for example when you are looking at the time, I would like you to Google the number that appears and the words "numerology meaning."

Signs: Keep your eyes open, look for things that appear, and shouldn't be there like feathers, pennies, dimes, flickering lights, or any meaningful reminders of them.

Finding Purpose Again

If you are lucky, you can look around and see what you do have in your life. You may find there are people still here who love you. There may even be people still here who need you. And if you look back before this happened, deep inside yourself, you may find there were passions, dreams, and things you were into.

This is a time for your healing and slowly integrating things you like to do back into your life. Emotions can quickly become overwhelming because each passing moment we ruminate accumulates more pain.

I encourage you to think about how you best receive love, and give it to yourself. You can google the *"5 Love Languages"* free online quiz to find out how you receive love. Identify what you would love more of in your life, and then bring it into existence with your own action.

Finding a new purpose comes in baby steps. First, creating a schedule around healing and integrating activities with supportive friends and family. Then, trying some new things and getting back into the flow of life. Prioritizing your personal health and the healthy relationships you do have in your life.

When you are truly ready to put yourself out there again just ask yourself, "What would be the most fulfilling and rewarding way to spend my time?"

Summary

I remember the fear I felt when facilitating my first workshop for the Mothers of Veteran Suicide. The heaviness began to twist in my chest as I felt the endless abyss of sorrow, loss, and complex PTS. Silently, I thought, "My God, how is the light going to shine through this?"

Now for the rest of the story. This experience was the ultimate testament to something I've been saying for years: "The light never disappoints." In that workshop, when the sorrow arose from deep within the group, I embraced my tension, listened, and waited patiently for my intuition to kick in. I wanted to hug each of the moms for eternity, but I waited for spirit to do from inside their mind and body. The video testimonials and smiling pictures the next day amplified my faith in this work and motivated me to share it with you today.

The more you reframe the relationship from the physical plane to the spiritual plane, the more you will regain an emotional connection, and from time to time, you will feel their presence in your life.

As the relationship transitions from the physical to the spiritual, you will know this life is temporary, that there is a reality far beyond what human eyes can see, and that you can tap into your connection with them by loving yourself unconditionally.

There is no "closure" to this pain, but there is a new beginning. If you can imagine working for a company for a very long time and your very best friend there has been miserable at the job for years.

When that friend leaves for a better opportunity where they are happy, it's a hard adjustment, as we won't see them physically every day, but in some small way we can be happy for them because they are in a better place and no longer unhappy.

There is no analogy to properly portray your pain. The truth is, your loved one was in unbearable pain here; now they are free from the pain and they want you to be happy again. This was my best attempt to reach you without being on a coaching call or in a retreat with you.

Energetically, love is expansion and feels good because love is in alignment with the universe, as our universe is also expanding. Energetically, fear is constriction and feels painful because fear is not in alignment with the universe. This is why love will always win in the end, it's in alignment with the universe.

This world is temporary; your touch and breath are tethers to the present moment, where you can break free from all the painful things you feel and see.

I want you to reopen your heart because love is the frequency of eternity, and that is where you and all your loved ones will eventually be. This is the eternal safe place; where love transcends time and space. It is inside you.

Acknowledgements

I wrote this book for you and your pain. I wrote this book because the problem continues to rise, and I don't yet see the answer in the mainstream.

Another big motivation to write this book was seeing the efficacy of this work first hand for decades. I feel now is the time to share it. The techniques in this book have proven effective under extreme circumstances time and again. I only share what I know works.

I am sorry beyond words if you felt any part of this book was insensitive or minimized your pain. I can only imagine the gut-wrenching emotions you are living through. Please know my motivation is solely to help you and those around you.

Every person is different and will have their own unique healing journey. The general approach I laid out in this book works because I designed it based on sound principles of mind, body, and spirit.

God bless you and your family.

Sincerely,
Brett Cotter

brett@stressisgone.com

Resources

Mental Health Urgency: 988

Emergency: 911

National Domestic Violence Hotline: 800-799-7233

National Suicide Prevention Lifeline: 800-273-TALK (8255)

National Hopeline Network: 800-SUICIDE (800-784-2433)

Lifeline Crisis Chat (Live messaging): crisischat.org

Crisis Text Line: Text "START" TO 741-741

Self-Harm Hotline: 800-DONT CUT (800-366-8288)

Family Violence Helpline: 800-996-6228

Planned Parenthood Hotline: 800-230-PLAN (7526)

American Association of Poison Control Centers: 800-222-1222

National Council on Alcoholism & Drug Dependency Hope Line: 800-622-2255

National Crisis Line Anorexia and Bulimia: 800-233-4357

LGBT Hotline: 888-843-4564

TREVOR Crisis Hotline: 866-488-7386

AIDS Crisis Line: 800-221-7044

Veterans Crisis Line: veteranscrisisline.net

https://www.mentalhealth.va.gov/suicide_prevention/index.asp

Suicide Prevention Wiki: suicideprevention.wikia.com

FREE TRAINING

CERTIFICATIONS

MEMBERSHIP

COACHING

YEAR ROUND RELIEF THAT WORKS
www.StressIsGone.com

www.ingramcontent.com/pod-product-compliance
Lightning Source LLC
Chambersburg PA
CBHW051244120626
46547CB00014B/1794